Introduction
to the
2018 Values Voter Summit Edition

***

It's never too late!

I was watching an interview with Steve Bannon a few weeks ago where he was talking about the upcoming mid-term elections on November 6. He said, correctly, that these elections would be for the most part a referendum on the Trump presidency and its many major accomplishments.

I think there is a great deal of truth to that, but then he said, incorrectly, that **it is too late** to try to convince people that Trump is doing great and important things for America and the world. He said all that matters now is which side can energize its base most completely with a big turnout.

Steve, respectfully, you are flat wrong!!!
It's never too late!!! Because of the endless false and negative news stories on Donald Trump and this administration, many, indeed probably most, of Trump's detractors are simply misinformed. What we now know after 2016 is **the actual truth** is once **anyone** understands the dynamic of what Trump is

really about and what he is trying to do, they will get on the so-called "Trump train," even if they do not want to say it openly or to a pollster.

Why is this? If a pollster calls and asks you, "Are you going to vote for that racist, bigot, sexist, xenophobe Donald Trump?" Any normal person will respond at best with "I'm undecided" and at worst with "No way, man,"

Why is this? Because *if* you say you are going to vote for Trump or one of this people, that is like saying to the pollster you think that you think racism, bigotry, sexism, and xenophobia are good things! And no one wants to do that!

The British pollsters found the exact same thing to be the case with the 2016 Brexit vote, and for the same reasons. No one likes to be thought of as an extreme "far-right" nationalist and bigot just because they think that open borders and radical multiculturalism might not be such a good idea.

What's the point? Trump's patriotic and nationalist agenda of the rule of law and America-first is not radical and extreme at all! Rather, the fact is it is the Left and specifically the Democrats who are radical and extreme with their policies of sanctuary cities, open borders, radical multiculturalism, a false "living Constitution," Social Justice, irresponsible spending, and, in truth, **lawlessness** generally.

Mr. Bannon, it is *never* too late to educate!!!
Why? The future of this great nation and indeed of the entire world depends upon it! We simply must clarify the issues to people and correct the countless distortions being perpetrated about Donald Trump by the mainstream media. It can be done and it will be done! Never miss an opportunity!

All of the Great Issues of History are, incredibly, culminating this very hour in these very elections we face in November. These elections are not just a referendum on Donald Trump and his presidency, but a referendum of biblical proportions dealing major issues of good government and even of Bible prophecy because today's globalism, which Trump so strongly opposes, is in fact the end-time Babylon Beast of Revelation while the apostate mainline denominations with their one-world religion are clearly the enabling Whore of Babylon as the scarlet harlot riding on the Beast. What's new?

In my experience, for the Trump supporter, this seems pretty plausible, even probable, but for the Trump-hater and the deplorable-hater this seems far-fetched and not remotely possible.

Is there any middle ground here? Not really. Why? One either thinks Socialist Justice a good thing or one thinks its opposite classical Justice is a good thing, but it is one or the other with no middle ground. One thinks either free and sovereign states with the rule of law are a good thing or one thinks open borders with lawlessness are a good thing, but it is one or the other.

One thinks e pluribus unum with Liberty and Justice for all is a good thing or one thinks diversity with radical multiculturalism is a good thing, but it is one or the other.

One thinks there are many ways to God and all religions worship the same God but by a different name or one thinks Christ and Christ alone makes atonement for our sins while other religions worship false gods, but it is one or the other! There is *no* middle ground!

One thinks statesmanship and doing the Right thing are the point of good government or one thinks special interest group advantage of the mere politician is a good thing, but it is one or the other, and again, there is *no* middle ground.

Finally, one thinks fear God and keep His commandments to love God with all your heart, mind and soul and to love your neighbor as yourself are the point of life on this planet or one does not, and there is, yet again, *no* middle ground.

The Fifth Monarchists in founding America believed that the hour in history had come for the worldwide Reign of Christ to begin, and yet again, one is either with them and for them, or one is not.

UNDERSTANDING
Statesmanship

Classical Justice
versus
Social Justice

Frank N. Mitchell

This UNDERSTANDING booklet is part of a series of booklets on key issues of our time on the Reign of Christ at
www.ashiningcityonahill.org
www.reignofchrist.org
All booklets are available at amazon.com

August 2018

Preface

This UNDERSTANDING booklet is one in a series of booklets concerning **THE REIGN OF CHRIST** for our time and how that Reign plays out in all history and as foretold in the Bible.

The problem that I have encountered over the last 30 or 40 years is that Christians who think we should be praying and working for the Kingdom to come on Earth (in order to have the thousand year Reign of Christ in all its fullness) are generally Liberals and apostates who have a false and counterfeit Social Gospel and Social Justice message and understanding of the Kingdom come on Earth and of any possible millennial era of Christ.

On the other hand solid Bible-believing Christians, for a variety of reasons, often tend to be what are called amillennialists and premillennialists, and these folks generally think we are **not** to be praying or working for the Kingdom outside of some minor evangelism and works of charity. Their view is, tragically, that Jesus told us to hunker down in the churches and to wait for Him to return and for this current age to end or the world to end as we know it.

The practical importance of all of this cannot be overstated. It means few if any conservative Bible commentators are really thinking about what it would mean for the Kingdom of God to come on

Earth in all its fullness in the much prophesied worldwide Reign of Christ.

And to further complicate these matters there are many aspects to an actual Kingdom Era come here on planet Earth, and there are many obstacles to how such a Kingdom might well play out in actual history. And, finally, for a true Kingdom come on Earth there are many interrelated political, religious and economic difficulties and confusions in our time to be resolved and overcome.

Given this situation, each booklet in this UNDERSTANDING series tends to stand on its own in order to address some given specific problem or set of problems concerning a coming millennial era on Earth where we will see the nations or "kingdoms of this world become the kingdoms of our Lord and of His Christ."

In this coming time, *each shall know the Lord from the least to the greatest* and *the knowledge of God will fill the whole world as waters cover the sea*. And in this Kingdom time, we will see, worldwide, true worship of God in Spirit and Truth, and we will see all the nations in harmonious interaction in Peace, Justice, and Righteousness.

This will then be the much prophesied and long anticipated reign of the Son of David in a worldwide Reign of Christ.

Frank Mitchell

UNDERSTANDING
Statesmanship
Classical Justice *versus* Social Justice

Statesmanship is doing what is best for the country as a commonwealth. This in the Constitution is called the "general Welfare" or, that is, the common good for everyone. This is also called doing Justice for the nation as a whole in the national interest, while being a mere politician is doing what is best for one's self or for one's own special interest group at the expense of other groups or the larger society.

Ancient Political Science

These ideas about statesmanship and Justice actually go back to the beginning of political science in ancient Greece and Athens where we see the beginning of our modern day concepts of democracy. The ancient Greeks experimented with various forms of government in order to find the one that worked best to promote the Justice of the common good. Both Plato and Aristotle wrote on this subject extensively in an effort to come up with a form of government where each person in the body politic does his own particular work or craft in harmonious interaction, economically and otherwise, with all the other parts of the body politic. This is the same idea of the harmonious interaction of all the parts of the whole body that Paul will use for the desirable functioning of the church or Body of Christ with each member having his own particular spiritual gifts and ministry.

In the Just state this harmonious interaction creates the general Welfare where no one (by good laws) can take advantage of others, in effect, in an immoral manner. It is the statesman who makes these good laws in Wisdom to this harmonious interaction ends. And, indeed, the **harmonious (moral) interaction** of all the parts of the body in peace and prosperity is *also* a definition of **classical Justice**, as is **treating equals equally** and **getting one's appropriate due**.

What Aristotle concludes from looking at this situation is that if one has a good king interested only in the well-being of his city-state, nation or kingdom then that is **the best** form of government because the king is disinterested and can, as a sort of umpire, make sure no person or persons or group tries to exploit others. The problem, as Aristotle sees it, is that if one has a bad king, called a tyrant, he will make everything in his kingdom work simply to his own advantage and to the advantage of the immediate circle around him, and this says Aristotle, famously, is **the worst** form of government, a one-man tyranny, as it were.

However, Aristotle, as the Greeks generally, tended to see other forms of government to be almost inherently flawed. Why? In a democracy where all citizens vote, the tendency of the bulk of the people is to try to pull down upper classes who simply do not have the voting power to defend even their very legitimate interests. Further, in a democracy, there is a tendency for demagogues to arise and to promise the masses great benefits if the masses will just elect the demagogue, who in reality is not interested in the well-being of the nation but simply in acquiring his own power. From this the Greeks tended to conclude democracy is the worst form of government for promoting and securing the general Welfare or common good. And in a somewhat similar manner an oligarchy, that is, a rule by the upper classes, has a tendency to exploit the masses of people, with high interest rates, low wages, or whatever it can.

It was from this mess that Plato famously came up with his utopian republic to be ruled by disinterested philosopher-kings. Plato's republic was not even remotely realistic or desirable, but his motive was to have a government that promotes the general Welfare of society and the harmonious interaction of all people where no one or any one group takes advantage of other people and other groups. Aristotle is much more level-headed about this whole situation, and he concludes **a mixed form of government (of monarchy, oligarchy and democracy) is the best**, and it has all groups represented to make sure they are all truly each seeking the general Welfare and not their own unfair advantage.   And, in fact, with time the **ancient Roman republic** will achieve this mixed form of government as will the **Glorious Revolution** in the UK and the **American Revolution** in the US.

How does this work? The House of Representatives or House of Commons is like a democracy, and the Senate or House of Lords in like an oligarchy, and the president or prime minister is like a king or chief executive officer. The ancient Roman republic had an assembly of the people and a senate of the upper classes and two consuls as chief executive officers. The key point here is each of these different branches of government is to be seeking the general Welfare or common good and not merely its own advantage, and each branch can offset the power of any other branch that tries to seek it own unjust advantage.

The long and the short of this is there are two types of government, namely, good and bad government. Good government seeks what is best for the nation as a whole, and bad government seeks the injustice of what is best for special interest groups. And the best way to good government is to have a system that has all groups represented in what Aristotle called mixed government as will be seen in the ancient Roman republic and in the constitutional monarchy of the Glorious Revolution and the constitutional republic of the American Revolution, with all three of them **being based on the moral Laws of Nature and of Nature's God, Wisely applied by the statesman legislator for the good of the whole nation as a commonwealth in harmonious interaction.**

The Glorious Revolution, American Revolution, and Marx

After the Roman republic, the Roman empire that followed it was an absolute monarchy, and in Western civilization absolute monarchy will continue to be the norm where the king's word is law and there are few if any rights for the people. This is why the Magna Carta of 1215 was such an important occurrence. However, it was the combination of the Glorious Revolution and the American Revolution (both with consent of the governed and equal rights for all based on the moral Natural Law as outlined by John Locke) that set a new standard in achieving Just and Righteous government using a mixed government model. The American republican model in particular became the model that many of the nations of the world would aspire to, the degree to which they were trying to transition out of some form of tyranny or absolute monarchy.

In fact, Jefferson called America the world's "best hope" for good government, and Lincoln went further than that and called America the world's "last best hope." However, for a variety of reasons, Karl Marx decided the Glorious Revolution and American Revolution (both based on the Higher Moral Law to do Justice for the common good) were all wrong, and Marx decided those revolutions were revolutions that were simply interested in furthering and legitimizing capitalist exploitation. So, Marx sought to have worldwide communist revolutions to end capitalism, free enterprise, all individual rights, all moral values, and ultimately all nation-states. Marx was a tyrannical collectivist and in the tradition of atheistic and hedonistic Epicurean-materialist humanism, and Marx felt that the family and family moral values were also a creation of the capitalist to maintain the capitalist system just as the free sovereign state was with classical Liberty and Justice for all.

As a materialist-humanist atheist it was self-evident to Marx that there was no God and no Higher Moral Law. In fact Marx is generally seen to be contemptuous of both the idea of God and the Higher Moral Law. And, further, Marx did *not* believe in **Social Justice** as later Marxist collectivists will. Marx believed there is to be a violent revolution by the proletariat to take over and set up a "dictatorship of the proletariat" government to appropriate all wealth to itself. This really had nothing to do with Justice or injustice.

Marx had a system that was based on hatred of the capitalist bourgeoisie and on violent class conflict and class resentment and so forth. The famous non-violent "third way" communists who come after Marx *also* seek to have a communism, but it is to be established by voting and not by violence. However, **it was to be the exact same communism.** This "third way" communism was to be based on a false love and a false moral standard of the universal brotherhood of man, which held that each person of all humanity on planet Earth has a "positive right" to an equal share of the world's wealth and resources.

Socialist "Justice"

When one gets one's equal share of the world's wealth in a non-violent "third way" communism as a supposed moral right or basic "human right," that is called socialist "Justice" or "Social Justice." The importance of this cannot be overstated. Why? Because **Social Justice theories give classical Marxism a moral justification, albeit a false one**. And this moral deception then gives the non-violent communist the moral high ground in education, law, government and the churches against the *supposed* clear moral evils of capitalism, private property, and traditional individual rights and liberties, which *supposedly* do nothing but exploit people, and steal their surplus labor value, etc., etc.

The highly esteemed C. S. Lewis said that it is the devil's goal (quite literally) to get all churches to preach the clear evils of Social Justice economics and government **as goods and as the point of the Christian faith**, which in fact will happen, and it is seen in our current Great Apostasy, which is primarily about a false Jesus and a false Gospel. However, in ancient philosophy and in the Bible, classical Justice and Righteousness make for good government and for good economics, and **classical Justice and Righteousness are the point of the Christian faith after salvation**.

In fact and in short, **Social Justice** is a *false* moral justification and a demonic deception for promoting the evil of communism in a generally non-violent manner at the voting booth. This means churches, schools, and various social and political groups who would never have promoted a violent hate-filled revolution to seize all the wealth of the capitalists will gladly and enthusiastically vote for the exact same agenda to seize and redistribute all the wealth of the capitalists in the name of a false brotherly love and Social Justice. This is an outrageous demonic deception and confusion, but it happens nonetheless in the West with the socialist or social democracy movement and the positive rights movement in the UK and US in the Labour and Democratic parties.

In fact, this demonic Social Justice communist nonsense is the whole point of having a socialist democracy, where people are to be educated (actually indoctrinated) in the schools and churches so they will vote for the worldwide communist agenda of worldwide Social Justice and its wealth redistribution in order to make us all economically equal and in order to end all borders, nation-states, and all traditional concepts of Liberty, Justice and Righteousness and even the liberty to speak about such things! In the collectivist tradition of Marx, these socialist democrats (or, that is, non-violent communists) hate virtually everything that is Good, True, and Right associated with God and classical Justice and Righteousness and even associated with

16

common sense, let alone the general Welfare and individual rights and liberties.

In the 20th century these so-called "social democrats" implement this hatred and the false moral theory of Social Justice first in the UK and then in the US by doing two things: first, either throwing out a Creator God altogether (of atheism) or, if not doing this atheism, they throw out classical concepts of God (for false demonic ones) and secondly in either case by also throwing out classical concepts of the moral Laws of Nature and of Nature's God because traditional concepts of God and the Higher Moral Law are seen as supposedly self-evidently false and even absurd!!!

And so, although it is by the vote and not violence, the social democrats, just as Marx, actually want to overthrow both **the Glorious and American Revolutions**, which were both based on the idea that the moral Laws of Nature and of Nature's God are self-evidently true and not self-evidently false.

Adding Social Justice to Classical Justice
It is no great insight for the socialist democrats to see that their ideas are not going to sell too well with the voting public in order to pull off their non-violent communist revolution at the ballot box. So, what the social democrats say is they want to leave in place the Glorious and American Revolutions and then **add to them theories of Social Justice and positive rights** for an equal share of the world's wealth and

resources. In fact, FDR did this openly and famously in his positive rights speech of 1944 where he established by mere proclamation, no less, a so-called "second bill of economic rights" to be **added** to the first Bill of Rights!!! This was totally outrageous, but it was done by him, he said, as an addition and a supposed completion for our times of the original Bill of Rights and Constitution.

However, one *cannot* add a second positive bill of Social Justice rights to traditional concepts of rights and to traditional concepts of Justice and Righteousness without negating the traditional concepts of rights to property and without negating Justice and Righteousness in order to implement the new *added* agenda of Social Justice and its positive rights to an equal share, etc. Why is this? This is not complicated.

The Preamble to the US Constitution says a central purpose of the US government is to "establish Justice" and "promote the general Welfare" among other things. A classic definition of Justice is one gets to keep the fruit of one's labors. This is not just common sense and in the natural revelation; it is even in the Bible. (Isaiah 3:10) Further, traditionally it is even a central function of the state **to protect property** while the entire point of Socialist Justice is that one does *not* deserve to keep the fruits of one's own labor, rather someone else deserves those fruits, and it is, therefore, the central job of the state to appropriate all the fruits of everyone's labor to itself and to redistribute those fruits equally among all the people, whether they work or not. This is doing Social Justice.

In short, **classical Justice** is actually **the complete opposite** of **Socialist Justice**. So, once one adds a list of Social Justice entitlement positive rights to the Constitution, the new added agenda of the US government becomes the exact opposite of the founding vision of Liberty and Justice for all traditionally or classically defined.

This is done *without* explicitly denouncing Liberty and Justice for all and traditional rights, but these things are all practically speaking displaced for the new entitlement-state, positive-rights, Social-Justice agenda of FDR. This new agenda is seen to be the new **moral** purpose of the state for those enlightened or educated enough to see the supposed brilliance and moral brilliance of worldwide Social Justice and the whole worldwide globalist agenda of one-world government, open borders, tolerance, hedonism, and unconditional agape love as license, lawlessness and indulgence based on the universal brotherhood of man, which is the single phony moral standard of the social democrats, where each person has an equal right to an equal share of the world's wealth.

The United Nations Charter and the Universal Declaration of Human Rights
This outrageous Social Justice non-violent communism of the socialist democrats is actually all

written into the United Nations Charter and the Universal Declaration of Human Rights and other UN documents, which also add in a basic human right to worship God however one wants to throughout the whole world, if one is inclined to be religious. In short, the atheist social democrats in order to sell their Social Justice agenda add a freedom of religion to their communism in a way that Marx would never have done, but this freedom of religion is just as phony as the politically correct freedom of speech and press the socialist democrats advocate. Why? Because one does not have the freedom to speak traditional notions of good and right and traditional notions of God because they are divisive of the universal brotherhood of man and his world unity. Speaking against the evil of the one-world socialist government and the evil of a false one-world religion is therefore hate speech and a violation of the basic human rights of all mankind.

This makes complete sense because if one has a basic human right to an equal share of the world's wealth and resources and a basic human right to live in a world free of nation-states, then anyone who says you do not have these rights is undermining basic human rights to these things. And the freedom to worship the non-existent God of all religions, a "God" of tolerance, utopian compassion and universal brotherhood supposedly worshipped by all religions, is hardly the freedom to worship the God of Abraham, Isaac, and Jacob who created the universe and who sent his Son to die on the Cross for our sins! In fact, that Christian freedom of worship is explicitly *not* a part of the New World Order of the one-world government of the United Nations and its Social Justice agenda and its false human rights agenda.

Why is that? Because the Creator God of Abraham, Isaac, and Jacob is a God of total Righteousness and Justice and divisive Judgment, all of which are by definition self-evident evils for the Liberal Social Justice Warrior as the very point of his Liberalism in his rejecting the Creator God of the Declaration of Independence as well as the moral Laws of Nature and of Nature's God.

The Two Great Falsehoods and the One-World Religion
The apostate Christian Liberal often says openly he wants to throw out the Two Great Commandments which are love God with all your heart, mind and soul, and love your neighbor as yourself (**which together give God and a Higher Moral Law**).

The Liberal wants to replace the Two Great Commandments with the Two Great Falsehoods of the universal fatherhood of God and the universal brotherhood of man. This is in addition to rejecting traditional doctrinal fundamentals and replacing them with new false fundamentals, such as the bodily Resurrection of Christ did not occur but his spirit lives on, and Christ did not die on the Cross to reconcile us to God but to each other and establish an inclusive radical multiculturalism, etc.

Pretty obviously such outrageous changes are not going to fly in many churches as a replacement theology or as replacement teachings and doctrine. So, just as political Liberals do with their positive rights agenda, the religious Liberals take their Two Great Falsehoods and their false atoning work of Christ (to reconcile mankind to himself supposedly) and they **add** them to traditional Christianity and its Two Great Commandments and its atoning work of Christ for our sins. And just as adding positive rights Social Justice to the US Constitution negates the Constitution, so too the Two Great Falsehoods, as the supposed new purpose of Christianity for today, negate the historical faith and its God and its Higher Moral Law. And adding a supposed atoning work of Christ to reconcile mankind to himself negates an atoning work of Christ to reconcile man to God.

With these negating additions to Christianity, the Liberal apostates have in practical fact created the one-world religion that holds all religions worship the exact same God (universal Father) but by a different name, and the new "moral" purpose of this new "Christianity" becomes exactly the same as that of the one-world government. It is the Social Justice agenda of the Social Democrats because the new "Christianity" has the exact same "moral" standard, namely, the universal brotherhood of man which creates an equal right to an equal share of the world's wealth in Socialist Justice.

To these political ends of one-world Social Justice government, the United Nations is specifically formed, which is a little known fact, and to these religious ends of a one-world religion worshipping the (demonic) God of all religions, the Protestant World Council of Churches is formed, and later the Catholics do a similar thing with Vatican II.

When these political and religious occurrences happen, the formation of the United Nations fulfills the prophecies of Revelation's **Babylon** officially attempting to control all economics, speech and thought (supposedly morally justified because of the universal brotherhood of man), and the World Council of Churches and Vatican II fulfill Revelation's **Whore of Babylon** with its apostate Liberal Christianity and its one-world religion based on the universal fatherhood of God and the universal brotherhood of man.

Mankind's Hour of Decision
So, it is decision time for humanity on Earth; take your pick: Will it be a **true statesmanship** of free sovereign states based on classical Justice and Righteousness with equal individual rights and liberties for all based on the moral Laws of Nature and Nature's God, Wisely applied by the statesman legislator for the common good of the nation as a commonwealth? Or will it be a **false statesmanship**

of *no* sovereign nation-states with a one-world government doing an evil worldwide Social Justice with no traditional individual rights and liberties for anyone and no Higher Moral Law and no actual Creator God of that Moral Law, all of which is generally openly advocated as a false moral high ground by the Democrat Party in the US and the Labour Party in the UK? For this writer, this is not a very tough call.

At this time, the future of the entire world for the next thousand years is not a matter of life or death; it is only a matter of people getting off their lazy duffs and going out to vote against any and all Democrats in the US and any and all Labour Party candidates in the UK with their self-proclaimed positive-rights Social-Justice agenda for all the nations of the world.

In my opinion, our children and grandchildren and their children and grandchildren after them will curse the day we were born if we in our two great nations screw this up, which we were usually in the process of doing until Brexit and Trump came along. However, if we can, at the ballot box, push Brexit and the Trump agenda through to successful completions, we can end the false **Social Justice globalist** agenda of the Left and thereby reestablish the nation-state based on **Liberty and Justice** for all as the model for all nations of the world for the coming millennium. This will be true statesmanship for the common good or general welfare, but it must be Wisely done.

Solomon prayed for Wisdom to be such a good king, and we in our time should pray to God to have a similar statesmanship Wisdom to legislate and even to vote for candidates to this ends. Scripture is quite clear (in Proverbs 8) that Wisdom *is* the Second Person of the Trinity and that Wisdom *is* the Logos of God (John 1).

This means that true Wisdom is actually the living Presence of God in us as individuals and in us as true statesmen. And James even says, in Christ, we are to ask God for such Wisdom, and He will give it to us generously. In the end this means that we are *literally* in the realm of the spirit sharing the throne with Christ and that Christ is Lord over the nations for Good, Just, and Right government in and through the saints.

===

Other booklets on the Reign of Christ in this UNDERSTANDING Series:

UNDERSTANDING Prophecy Fulfillment:
The Great Apostasy, Babylon, Mystery Babylon & the Reign of Christ

This little booklet gives an overview of the central major prophecies concerning the possible soon coming Reign of Christ. Specifically these are the prophecies of the Great Apostasy, Babylon, Mystery Babylon, and the man of lawlessness. These prophecies are seen as fulfilled in the false millennial visions of Marx and of the New World Order of UN Agenda 21 and Agenda 2030 and in the Liberal World Council of Churches.

UNDERSTANDING All Bible Prophecy:
Genesis to Revelation

This booklet holds that all prophecy should be interpreted in terms of the larger story of the Bible and the larger story of the Christian cosmology from the Creation to the Final Judgment, and this is especially the case for the book of Revelation.

UNDERSTANDING Globalism:
What is the "New World Order"?

This booklet looks at what "globalism" is generally and at the related topic of a "New World Order" that actually has *very* specific definitions and formulations that are often not well-known.

UNDERSTANDING Revelation 19:
Victory over One-World Government and One-World Religion

Revelation 19 though very controversial is actually very straightforward. The saints in a Marriage Supper of the Lamb move into a new more mature, intimate, and complete relationship with Christ, and then the saints in Christ and Christ in the saints completely and totally defeat the evils of one-world government and one-world religion. Simple enough when you get right down to it.

UNDERSTANDING Statesmanship
Classical Justice *versus* Social Justice

Probably no two notions are more misunderstood as well as more necessary to understand in our time than classical Justice and Social Justice. This booklet looks at the history of these two terms and how one stands for the Justice of statesmanship for doing the common good and the other for the injustice of special interest groups and wealth redistribution as a false human right for economic equality.

UNDERSTANDING Alternative Political Universes:
The Natural Revelation & Self-Evident Truths

For some folks as Jefferson and the American founders, the Natural Law or so-called Higher Moral Law is a self-evident truth, but for others with a reprobate mind and no common sense, this is not the case at all. These modern-day people who have lost their common sense are just as the ancient Epicureans (atheist hedonists) while modern-day Liberals are just as ancient Gnostics with their false enlightenment and false morality. Understand these things, and you will pretty well understand Alternative Political Universes.

UNDERSTANDING Illegal Immigration:
The Wall and All It Stands For

"The Wall" of Donald Trump stands for many larger issues from exposing hypocrisy among professional politicians to ending globalism, open borders, and the often total lawlessness of our time. Lawlessness of the Liberal and atheist-humanist is, in fact, the spirit of anti-Christ.

UNDERSTANDING The Whole Counsel of the Kingdom:
The Central Message of Jesus and Paul

Both Jesus and Paul preached a Whole Counsel of the Kingdom message, but this is not a generally well-known truth. This booklet looks at the concept of a Whole Counsel of the Kingdom Christianity and what it entails, namely, true worship of God in Spirit and Truth as well as Just and Righteous government.

UNDERSTANDING Spiritual Warfare:
Satan as a Roaring Lion

Scripture tells us that Satan goes about like a roaring lion seeking whom he may devour, but this is generally not a very understood warning, and tragically many people, if not devoured completely, get an arm or leg eaten (so to speak). To be forewarned is to be forearmed. This booklet deals with ways to recognize and deal with demons.

===

All of the above booklets are part of a series on key issues of our time on the Reign of Christ at
www.ashiningcityonahill.org
www.reignofchrist.org

All of the above booklets are put together is a single **Volume I** called

UNDERSTANDING
The Reign of CHRIST
The One Big Issue of Our Time
Volume I

This Volume I of all the above booklets together as well as all of the above booklets separately are available at **amazon.com**